Stripes

Devised by Monica Hughes

Collins

6

10

Stripes

Ideas for guided reading

Learning objectives: track the text (photographs) in the correct order; talk about the text identifying major points and key themes; locate significant parts of the text using photographs; interact with others, negotiating plans and activities and taking turns in conversation.

Curriculum links: knowledge and understanding of the world: investigate objects, materials, living things, similarities, differences, patterns and change

Getting started

- Show the children something with stripes (e.g. a straw or a scarf). Introduce the word *stripe*. Can the children see any other stripes in the room?

- Look at the striped clothes on the front cover of the book together. Identify some of the colours that make the stripes. Read the title together.

- Look carefully at pp2–3. If necessary, introduce the word *zebra*. Ask the children to match the stripes on pp2 and 3. Ask the children to describe the stripes (introduce words for colour and shape, e.g. *thick, thin, bendy, straight*).

- Show the children p4 only, covering p5 and the bit of the animal on p4. Ask the children to predict what the striped thing is (a snake). In pairs, ask the children to describe the snake's stripes to each other.

Reading and responding

- Walk through each of the pages to p13, and introduce new vocabulary. Encourage the children to turn the pages with you in order.

- On each new spread ask the children, in pairs, to find the stripes in the larger picture.

- Encourage the children to look at each picture carefully. Ask questions to help the children to describe the stripes using the pictures. Provide new vocabulary where necessary to help the children discuss their ideas.